This book belongs to:

....

....

BIRDS AND FLOWERS COLORING BOOK FOR ADULTS

Birds And Flowers coloring book help you be creative with the same colors and drawings with cute and funny pictures. Practice the dexterity of the hands and how to appraise the delicate color of the brain. Help improve the ability to think images, colors, concentration and you form a clear, vivid worldview. The book with a nice eye design, a graphic image would have brought you the interest.

Deidre Motys is a publisher of fun and relaxing coloring books for kids and adults. Be sure to check out other unique and creative titles.

Happy Coloring!

BIRDS AND FLOWERS COLORING BOOK FOR ADULTS

BIRDS AND FLOWERS COLORING BOOK FOR ADULTS

BIRDS AND FLOWERS COLORING BOOK FOR ADULTS

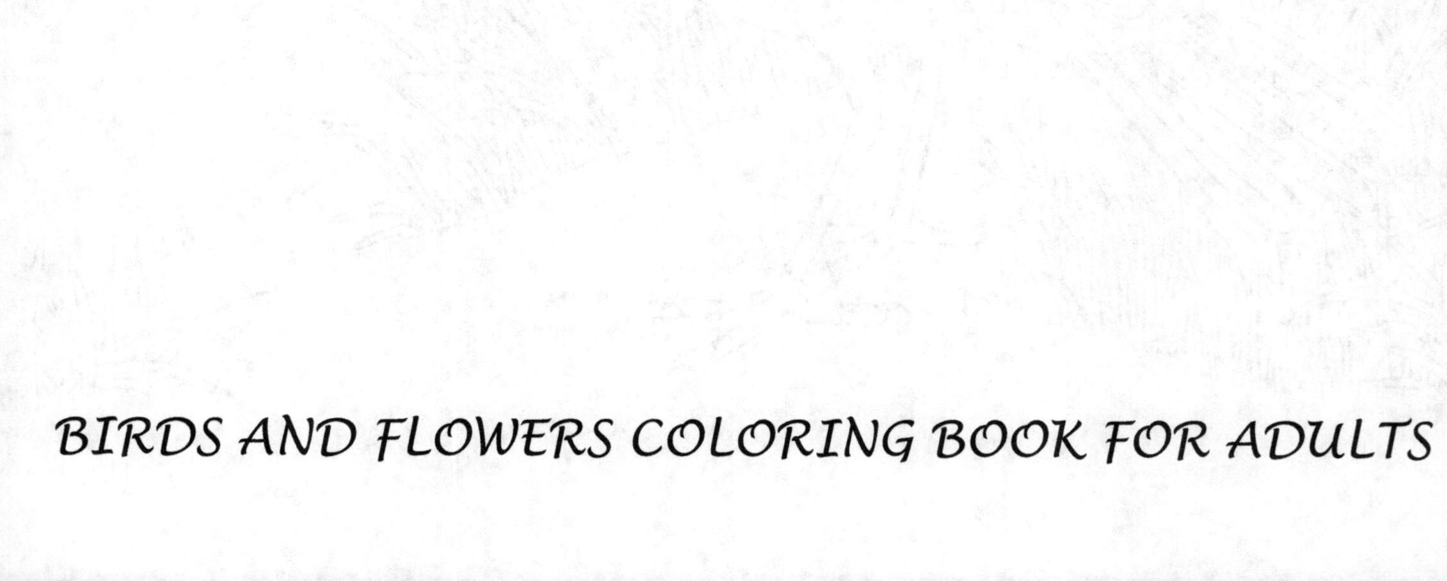

BIRDS AND FLOWERS COLORING BOOK FOR ADULTS

BIRDS AND FLOWERS COLORING BOOK FOR ADULTS

BIRDS AND FLOWERS COLORING BOOK FOR ADULTS

BIRDS AND FLOWERS COLORING BOOK FOR ADULTS

BIRDS AND FLOWERS COLORING BOOK FOR ADULTS

BIRDS AND FLOWERS COLORING BOOK FOR ADULTS

BIRDS AND FLOWERS COLORING BOOK FOR ADULTS

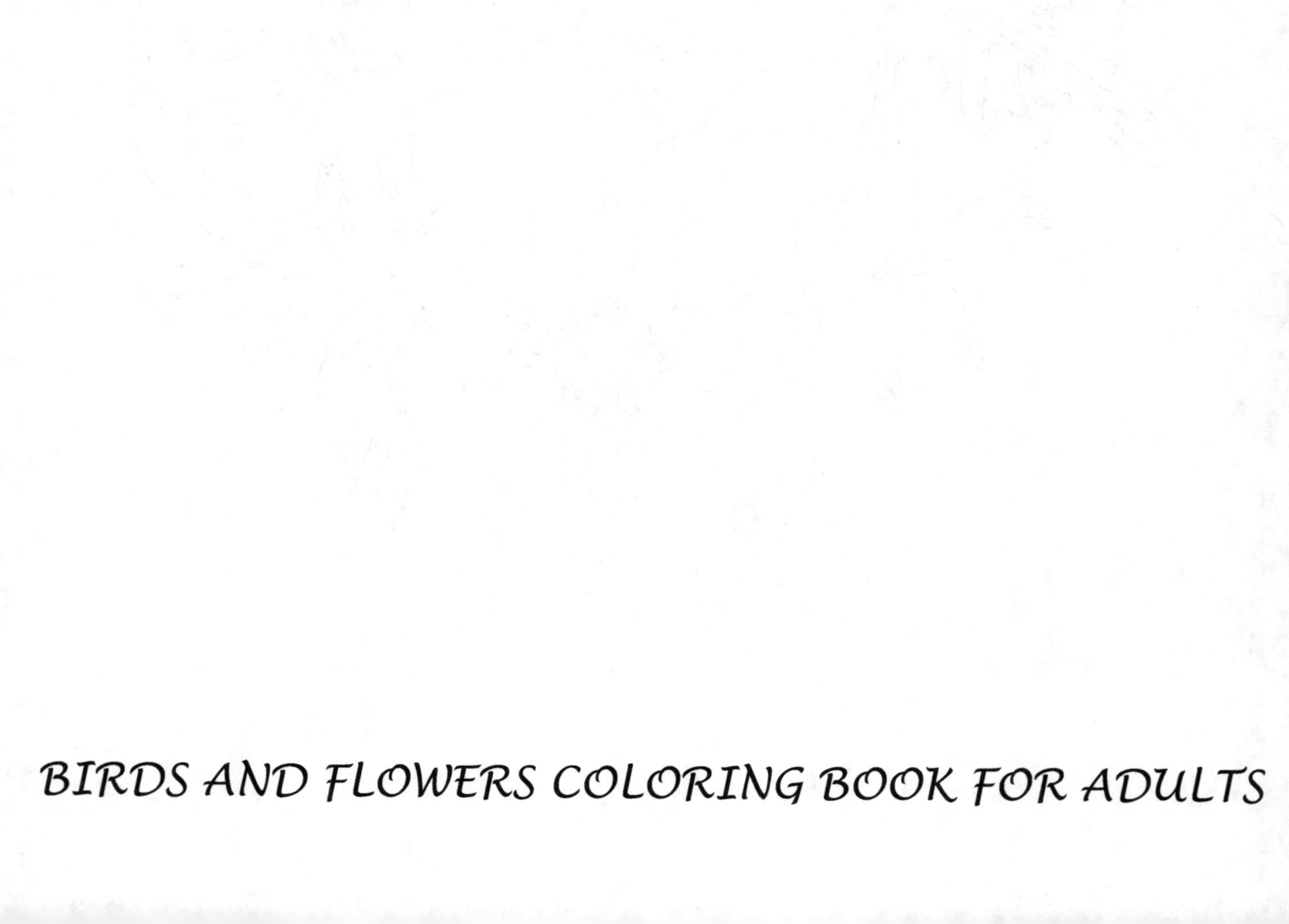

BIRDS AND FLOWERS COLORING BOOK FOR ADULTS

BIRDS AND FLOWERS COLORING BOOK FOR ADULTS

BIRDS AND FLOWERS COLORING BOOK FOR ADULTS

BIRDS AND FLOWERS COLORING BOOK FOR ADULTS

BIRDS AND FLOWERS COLORING BOOK FOR ADULTS

BIRDS AND FLOWERS COLORING BOOK FOR ADULTS

BIRDS AND FLOWERS COLORING BOOK FOR ADULTS

BIRDS AND FLOWERS COLORING BOOK FOR ADULTS

BIRDS AND FLOWERS COLORING BOOK FOR ADULTS

BIRDS AND FLOWERS COLORING BOOK FOR ADULTS

BIRDS AND FLOWERS COLORING BOOK FOR ADULTS

BIRDS AND FLOWERS COLORING BOOK FOR ADULTS

BIRDS AND FLOWERS COLORING BOOK FOR ADULTS

BIRDS AND FLOWERS COLORING BOOK FOR ADULTS

BIRDS AND FLOWERS COLORING BOOK FOR ADULTS

BIRDS AND FLOWERS COLORING BOOK FOR ADULTS

BIRDS AND FLOWERS COLORING BOOK FOR ADULTS

BIRDS AND FLOWERS COLORING BOOK FOR ADULTS

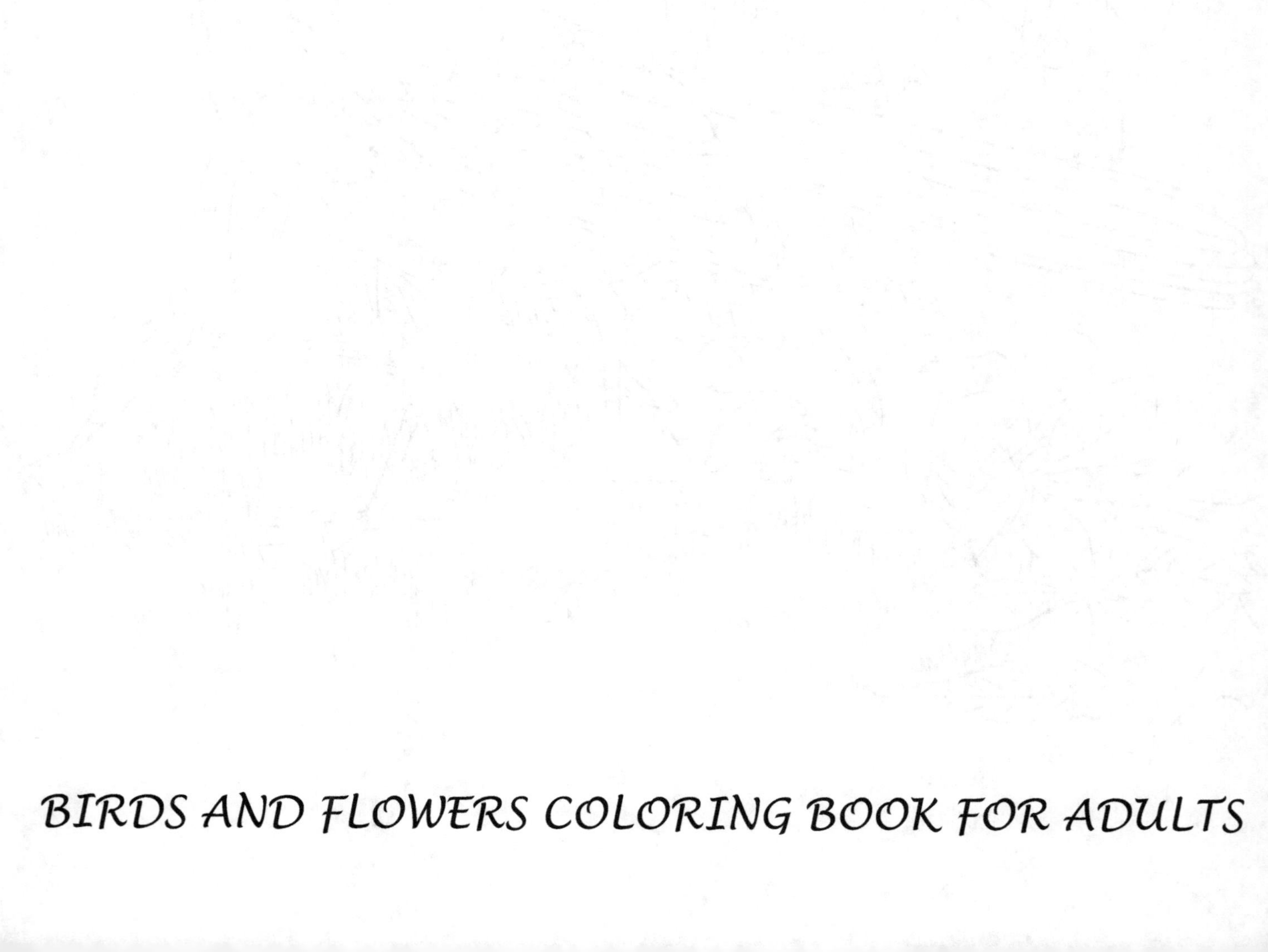

BIRDS AND FLOWERS COLORING BOOK FOR ADULTS

BIRDS AND FLOWERS COLORING BOOK FOR ADULTS

BIRDS AND FLOWERS COLORING BOOK FOR ADULTS